Canadian
"The Little Iron Horse"
For Kids

Nature Books for Kids
By
K. Bennett

JD-Biz Publishing

Read More Amazing Animal Books

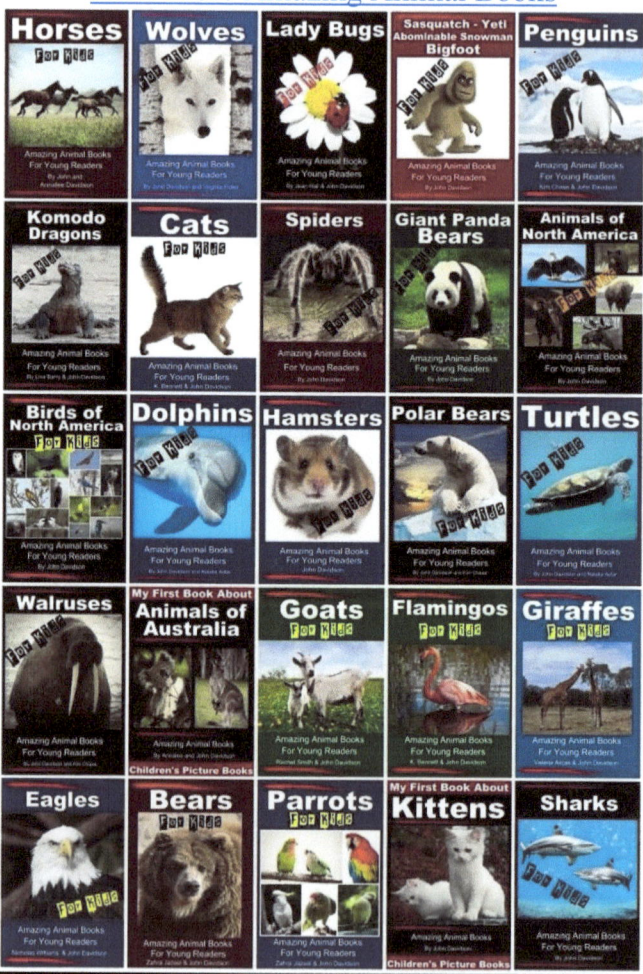

Purchase at Amazon.com

Table of Contents

Introduction

Author Bio

Introduction

***

Canadian Horse: The Canadian horse is a very special horse that comes from Canada. They descend from draft and light riding horses and have beautiful colors like black, bay, brown and chestnut. It is a very sturdy horse.

What does "sturdy" mean?

Vocabulary.com says "sturdy" means: firm, steady and tough. So this horse is strong and can do lots of hard work. Do you remember what draft horses are?

A draft horse.

This is a horse that "draws" or "hauls" something. It is also called a work horse or heavy horse, because it works hard and pulls heavy loads. However, these types of horses are usually strong, gentle, easy to work with and very patient.

Many years ago, there were three different types of the Canadian horse called: Canadian heavy draft (draft type) or St. Lawrence, Canadian

Frencher (trotting type) and Canadian Pacer (pacing type). Do you know what this means?

*A **draft horse type***: Remember: draft horses were used as work horses. So these horses were great at helping farmers to do hard work.

*A **trotting type:*** This means the horse walks in a certain way. It's called a gait. This type of movement is diagonal. So the horse moves its right front leg and left hind together. Then it moves its left front leg and right hind together.

*A **pacing type***: To get this type of walk the horse moves its right front and right hind together. And then it moves its left front and left hind together. This is called a lateral walk.

If you want to get a clue on how this is done try to walk like this: Move your RIGHT HAND and LEFT FOOT together and then move your LEFT HAND and RIGHT FOOT together. That's diagonal.

Now move your RIGHT HAND and RIGHT FOOT together. Then move your LEFT HAND and LEFT FOOT together. That's lateral.

Did you get it? Good job!

Canadian Horse

What makes this horse so special?

The Canadian horse is a rare breed. This means the horse is not well known. Have you ever heard of a Canadian horse before? If you have, great! If you haven't heard of them, this will be a nice way to learn more about this beautiful creature. Don't forget to share what you learn with others. Remember: Sharing is caring!

HOW TO DRAW A SIMPLE HORSE FOR KIDS:

Would you like to learn how to draw a horse? Wikihow.com has a simple, but neat tutorial. Here are the steps to get started:

1- First, ask your parent's or a guardian's permission to go online.

2- In your browser (Chrome, Internet explorer, Firefox, Torch) type: www.Wikihow.com

3- In the search box at the top of the page type: *Draw a simple horse*. Once the search is complete, you should see a title that reads: **"How to draw a simple horse: 11 steps with pictures."**

4 – Click on the link and follow the steps.

5- Have fun!

Canadian Horse

Chapter 1

Hellooooooo!

History: To understand where this beautiful horse comes from, we have to go back in history to the time of a King called Louis XIV or Louis the great.

Who was Louis XIV?

This King is called the Sun King, and he ruled for a very long time. 72 years and 110 days! It seems the King really loved horses and he sent some of them to Canada.

Gentleman farmers were allowed to get the horses to help them work but it was hard on the poor animals. Why? The working conditions were tough. Winter was a very hard time for the horses and they had to work long hours and there wasn't much food to eat. The strength and energy to endure harsh conditions gave the Canadian horses the nicknames: "Le Petit Cheval de Fer," which means: "little iron horse" or "horse of steel."

After some time, this strong little horse started to grow in numbers and moved around the country. Some even escaped and became feral horses. Do you remember what feral means?

What is a feral horse?

This horse is usually called a "wild horse." It roams freely but it wasn't born that way. It comes from domesticated horses that were owned by someone. Usually, these horses escaped their owners and ended up living "in the wild."

Hi there!

Numbers

The Canadian horse grew into big numbers and by 1849 there were more than 150,000 horses! Many of the horses went to the USA and were used for racing, pulling wagons and stagecoaches.

The horses were also used in the American Civil War. The horses were so important to the soldiers that many thought the North won the war because of the horses! Sadly, many of these beautiful animals died and by 1880, the Canadian horse had fallen in numbers. They were almost extinct! By the 1970's there were about 400 horses around the world and then something amazing happened!

In 1987, a Canadian horse team won the North American Drive Championship. This caused many people to believe in the Canadian horse again! And in 2002, the Canadian horse heritage and preservation society was formed. Can you guess why? Yes! To protect and preserve the Canadian horse.

Today, the Canadian horse is the national horse of Canada! Would you like to get one?

Shhh... I'm going to jump the fence.

Canadian Horse

How big are they?

Canadian horses are between 14 – 16 hands. This does not mean some are not taller but this is the standard size.

How much do they weigh?

They weigh between 1,000 and 1,400 pounds. The average weight for a stallion is: 1,050 to 1,350 pounds and the average weight for a mare is: 1,000 to 1,250 pounds.

How much do you weigh? Does the Canadian horse weigh more or less than you? How much more does it weigh? Do the math and find the answer!

I decided to stay inside!

Canadian Horse

This is a neat way to measure horses. The measurement refers to hands, literal hands!

Many years ago, people did not have rulers or measuring sticks like we do today. So they used whatever they had…and they had hands. So horses are measured in hands. You can do this too! One hand is 4 inches.

So if a horse is 15 hands multiply this by 4. (15 x 4) and you will get 60 inches. And if a horse is 16 hands multiply this number by 4. (16 x 4) and you will get 64 inches.

Now that you know how to do it, you can measure the other horses for yourself. Have fun!

This food is much better. Try a bite!

Strengths: Canadian horses are tough little creatures with a heart of gold. They are called an "all purpose" horse. This means they can do a little bit of everything! But for now, they are mostly used in riding and driving.

They are also called "easy keepers." This simple means they are easy to keep or care for!

The Canadian horse is also good at different types of discipline so they participate in many events for horses. Events like dressage and jumping. You probably know what jumping means but do you remember what dressage is?

Dressage training: Dressage training has been around for a very long time. The purpose of this training is to have your horse be the best it can be. The USDF (United States Dressage Federation) organization lists different levels for this type of skill. There are five levels:

-Training level

-First level
-Second level
-Third level
-Fourth level

Before you begin this type of training, there are several things to do. *Wikihow.com* suggests the following steps.

1- Both you and your horse need to know each other very well! And you need to know if you can trust each other. So a close relationship is very important before any training can begin!

2- You have to start to work on the way your horse walks or trots. This is referred to as a gait. It is very important for your horse to walk in the right way.

3- **Transitions:** This is when you want your horse to change from one movement to another. It is important that this step is done in a smooth manner. It should be just like putting one footstep in front of the other without tripping over your feet!

4- Your position in the saddle should look comfortable and balanced! And your heels should be down at all times.

5 – Practice makes perfect. To get good at any skill, you need to do it over and over again. Practicing with your horse is a great way to get good at riding him!

Of course there are many other steps to dressage that is very important. But these are some of the basic ideas. If you want to learn more, ask your parent or a guardian to help you research.

Weaknesses: Sadly, there are not many of these beautiful animals left and they are on the "critical" list. So if you wanted to get one, it might be a little difficult to find the "right" one.

The snow can't stop me!

CURIOUS FACT FOR KIDS:

There is a Canadian painter by the name of Cornelius Krieghoff who did beautiful paintings with the Canadian Horse. Can you guess what season out of the 4 seasons he chose as his favorite for his paintings?

a) Spring
b) Summer
c) Fall
d) Winter

If you are curious, ask your parent or a guardian to help you research the answer online. Share your findings with others!

Ready to train?

Training: Training a Canadian horse is like training other horse breeds. So let us detail the steps for training all horses to give you a better idea.

Wikihow recommends the following steps:

1-**First of all, don't scare the horse**. That means you should not run up or sneak up on them suddenly. This is not a hard to understand. For example, do you like it when people run or sneak up on you suddenly? It may scare you when someone does that, right? Then a horse will feel the same way.

2-*Be gentle and talk gently to your horse*. There is no need to yell, shout or talk in a harsh tone to your horse. Again, this idea is not hard to understand. Do you like it when people talk to you gently? Or do you want them to shout and yell at you? Isn't it nicer to treat others kindly and don't you appreciate it when others do the same for you? Your horse will appreciate your kind manner too!

3-*Most horses love to be touched*. Show them your feelings through your hands. Stroke them on the head, massage their neck, hug them, brush them and communicate your affection through gentle fingers. Imagine how happy your horse will be!

4-*Try to spend as much time as you can with your horse*. In any friendship, regular visits are the key! No matter what you have to do, stop by and visit your horse just to remind them that you're there. They will be so happy to see you and the more you spend time with them, the stronger your bond will grow.

5- *A nice reward*. A tasty treat, rub or pat down, yummy food, grooming of whatever other treat you might have in mind, will be a great idea! Do this at the end of the day to let your horse know how much you enjoyed spending time with them.

Royalgrovestables.blogspot.com notes another beautiful attitude of horses. It is their intuition or intuitive nature. This means a horse can *sense* your feelings, emotions and will react on those feelings.

If you are angry, upset, unhappy or grouchy, the horse will sense these negative feelings. This will not help you to get close to them. Instead, they may run away. But if you are positive, upbeat and happy then they will be happy to be around you. And it will be much easier to bond with them!

Chapter 2

Out for a walk!

Have you learned anything new about the Canadian horse? Wonderful! But there is still a little bit more we can learn.

Because of their good skills and strength, Canadian horses are used in trail riding and as a stock horse. Would you like to learn a little more about these skills?

Stock horse: A stock horse is very good with livestock, especially cattle (like cows). These types of horses can move quickly and have powerful back legs or hindquarters. They are also very smart with a "cow sense." This means they "know" how cows think so they can respond in the best way! The horse usually does this by themself so the rider doesn't have to do too much!

Think about it like this: Do you have a pet of some kind? If you do, can you guess what they are going to do BEFORE they do it? This is what the stock horse does with cows! Isn't that a smart horse?

Trail riding: Do you know what a trail is? *Kids.Net.Au* says it is a *"path or track through wild or hilly country."* So these paths or roads don't have cars on them. And some of these roads are very narrow with lots of trees, bushes and shrubs. Sounds like a jungle hmmm?

Many times people will ride their horses on these trails just for fun. But sometimes they do it for an event or competition. During competition, a trail becomes more than just a path! This is where endurance riding comes in. What's that?

Endurance riding: This depends on distance, trail and terrain. This simply means what the land looks like, if it has hills, curving snakelike roads, lots of rocks and things like that. Some of the competitive events are 25 miles long all the way to 100 miles! Do you think you could ride your horse for 100 miles?

Sometimes it does not matter which horse passes the finish line. What matters is how long it takes to ride that far. Sounds complicated? I think I would much rather ride for fun! What about you?

CURIOUS FACT FOR KIDS:

Horses, like us, have different titles for different stages of life. For example when a horse is born until 6 months of age it is called a *foal*.

Then up to the age of 2 years it is called a *yearling*. If the horse is a male horse it is called a *colt* under the age of 4. When it is older than 4 years it is called a *stallion*. Do you remember what a Stallion is?

Meaning of Terms:

A *stallion* is a: Male horse that can have kids.

A *gelding* is a: Male horse that cannot have kids. (Geldings are usually patient, calm, quiet and well behaved.)

A young female horse or pony is called *filly* and after the age of 4, she is called a *mare*. (Source: *Lessonpaths.com*)

Canadian Horse

Chapter 3

Here are a few additional facts about Canadian horses you may like to know.

-Canadian horses live for a long time. They are tough little horse with a big personality.

-Canadian horses learned to be tough. Many of them were left along to survive. During the summer, they ran loose in the forest. In the winter they were fed very little and they worked hard during the other months of the year. Many people thought this was the best way to help the horse get stronger.

-This horse is a warm blood. Do you remember the difference between a cold blood and a warm blood horse?

-The Canadian sport horse is a great horse for beginners but it is a little big! So it is recommended for a rider with a little more experience than a beginner.

- The Canadian horse is a light horse because of its weight. Do you remember how much it weighs? Light horses are usually less than 1,500 pounds. That's why the Canadian horse is light!

I'm just resting with my mommy!

These other facts refer to all horses and not just the Canadian horse. But I wanted to share them with you.

-Horses are great at keeping watch. It is rare to see a herd with everyone snoozing at one time. There is usually one horse standing as a lookout, and his job is to warn the others if danger comes near!

- Avoid standing behind a horse. They have great vision, but there are a couple of blind spots. Can you guess what the back part of the horse is? Yes! It's a blind spot. If the horse gets angry or scared, guess what he might do if you stand directly behind him?

-Horses are great at listening! They can turn their ears in different ways to improve their hearing. If you whisper and say something bad about your horse, they just might hear you!

- Horses can help people get better when they have mental or health problems. This is called: ***Equine Assisted Therapy***.

-Horses are the best sleepers on the planet. They can sleep lying down and standing up! Can you do that?

- Horses are herbivores. Do you know that this means? It means they eat plants or are plant eaters, if you like this term better.

Love you too!

GENERAL HORSE TIPS FOR KIDS:

It is important to care for your horse as you would any other creature. Here are some tips you can think about. These basic principles apply to most if not all horses. (Source: Frank Bell- *Horsewhisperer.com*)

-Your horse's diet is very important. Some horses have very hot blood and some have cooler blood. If your horse is hot blooded, they will need less protein in their diet. Do you remember what a Canadian horse is? Cold blood or warm blood?

-Learn how to properly discipline your horse. Remember: These animals are very sensitive. Let them know when they are getting too out of control! This can be done with a shhhhh noise or a firm tone to let them know who is in control.

-If the horse's head is high it means your horse is not relaxed. They may be upset in some way. If their head if low they are relaxed. Try to get your horse to stay relaxed. This will help them feel good and both of you will enjoy the ride.

-Horses love to get your tender rubs and soft pats. Things like rubbing their ears, nose, eyes and mouth is great. And a massage is even better!

-If a horse is trained really well, he or she will invite YOU for a ride. You should be looking for the invitation! Then you will enjoy an awesome ride.

-Your horse can sense your moods and behavior. If you are confident your horse will be confident too!

-You should feed your horse from a bucket and not your hand. (This is the recommendation, but I feel it is better to feed them with your hand from time to time! It seems to generate more trust and respect, but that is just my humble opinion on the subject. What do you think?)

Canadian Horse

CANADIAN SPORT HORSE TIPS FOR KIDS:

The Canadian Sport horse comes from a mix with Thoroughbreds, so this horse has special needs. Here is a short list to help you.

- They love discipline and exercise, so this is a great way to get your horse in shape and teach them how to behave!

- A box stall is a great choice for this type of horse but you need to turnout daily. This means your horse needs to get out of the stall every day. It needs to run free! Why? Think about this: Do you want to be stuck in one place every day without moving around? Neither does your horse! This will help to reduce their stress and make them feel happy.

-The Canadian sport horse eats a lot. So you will have to feed it a balanced diet. This means lots of fresh hay and grain but keep the carbohydrates low. Don't forget fresh tasting water too!

-It is a great idea to include vitamins and minerals. Your horse needs them to grow healthy and strong. (Source: *Horses.animal-world.com*)

Conclusion

In conclusion: Horses are beautiful creatures, and the Cheval Canadian (Canadian horse) is no exception. This patient, gentle, good natured horse is a wonderful example of how amazing Earth's creatures can be. Their rich history also teaches us how important this horse has been to many people for a long time. And today, this beautiful horse is still a part of Canada's natural heritage.

Although listed as critical, this is a great time to learn a bit more about these noble animals. You may be amazed at what you can discover. If you don't know exactly what to research about this noble breed, then think about this: Why don't you choose something you really like (It can be the tail, mane, ears, body, size, personality, history, etc) and learn a bit more about that particular subject?

If you are in school and you participate in show and tell, use that as your subject. Many of your classmates may not even know what a

---

Canadian Horse

Canadian horse is really like, so it would be nice to share what you find with others!

I hope this book has taught you just how wonderful nature is and how each creature can impact our life in amazing ways.

Canadian horses are a special part of nature's magnificent wonders. And so are you!

Author Bio

K. Bennett loves to write for both children and adults. Many different subjects are interesting to develop, but writing for children is special to her heart.

Her favorite pastimes include reading, traveling and discovering new things. Each of these activities helps to fuel her imagination and acts like a blank canvas waiting for more stories.

She is intrigued with fantasy elements like hidden worlds and faraway lands. Basically anything that gets her imagination soaring to new heights!

Her writing credits include children books online, short stories for online magazines, and two novellas listed at Amazon.com

Our books are available at

1. Amazon.com

2. Barnes and Noble

3. Itunes

4. Kobo

5. Smashwords

6. Google Play Books

Publisher

JD-Biz Corp

P O Box 374

Mendon, Utah 84325

http://www.jd-biz.com/

Canadian Horse

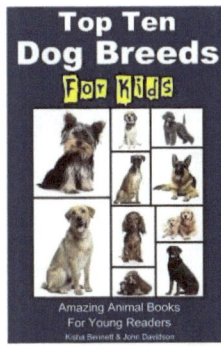

Top Ten Dog Breeds For Kids
Amazing Animal Books For Young Readers
Kisha Bennett & John Davidson

German Shepherds
Dog Books for Kids
K. Bennett

Bulldogs
Dog Books for Kids
K. Bennett

Dachshund
Dog Books for Kids
K. Bennett

Poodles
Dog Books for Kids
K. Bennett

Labrador Retrievers
Dog Books for Kids
K. Bennett

Rottweilers
Dog Books for Kids
K. Bennett

Boxers
Dog Books for Kids
K. Bennett

Golden Retrievers
Dog Books for Kids
K. Bennett

Puppies
Dog Books For Kids
Amazing Animal Books
By John Davidson

Beagles
Dog Books for Kids
K. Bennett

Yorkshire Terriers
Dog Books for Kids
K. Bennett

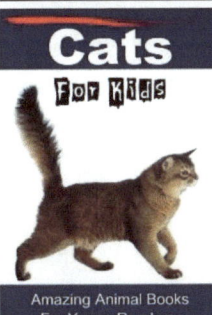

Dogs
Top Ten Dog Breeds For Kids
Amazing Animal Books For Young Readers
Zahra Jazeel & John Davidson

Cats For Kids
Amazing Animal Books For Young Readers
K. Bennett & John Davidson

Foxes For Kids
Amazing Animal Books For Young Readers
Zahra Jazeel & John Davidson

Wolves For Kids
Amazing Animal Books For Young Readers
By John Davidson and Virginia Fidler

Canadian Horse

Canadian Horse

www.ingramcontent.com/pod-product-compliance
Lightning Source LLC
Chambersburg PA
CBHW050911290526
45792CB00002B/778